Spell of the Ordinary

poems by

Jerome Gagnon

Finishing Line Press
Georgetown, Kentucky

Spell of the Ordinary

Copyright © 2018 by Jerome Gagnon
ISBN 978-1-63534-401-1 First Edition
All rights reserved under International and Pan-American Copyright Conventions. No part of this book may be reproduced in any manner whatsoever without written permission from the publisher, except in the case of brief quotations embodied in critical articles and reviews.

ACKNOWLEDGMENTS

My gratitude to the editors of those journals in which the following poems first appeared:

Self: *Xanadu*, Spring 2016
Spotting Turkeys; *Crossroads*, Vol. I., 2016
Cranking the Wheel: *Crab Creek Review*, Fall 2015
Joice Street Steps, Crossings: *Archaeopteryx*, 2014
Crow Makes a Scene: *Riverfeet Anthology*, 2017
Bonsai: *Roaring Muse*, 2017
First Frost: *Contemporary Poetry* – an Anthology of Present Day Best Poems, 2017 (Vol. 3)

Publisher: Leah Maines
Editor: Christen Kincaid
Cover Art and Design: Tony Sanchez
Author Photo: Mary Sanchez

Printed in the USA on acid-free paper.
Order online: www.finishinglinepress.com
          also available on amazon.com

                Author inquiries and mail orders:
                       Finishing Line Press
                           P. O. Box 1626
                     Georgetown, Kentucky 40324
                               U. S. A.

Table of Contents

Shed 1

Spotting Turkeys 2

Yellow House 3

Gifts 4

This Cup 5

Praise for Gray 6

Cranking the Wheel 7

Joice Street Steps 8

Barometer 9

Pulling Weeds 10

In the Lobby of Hotel Paradise 11

Laundry Day 12

Crow Makes a Scene 13

Still Life with Lemons 14

Praising Chair 15

Visitors 16

Evening Rain 17

Bonsai 18

Self 19

First Frost 20

Crossings 21

Something of What Was 22

SHED

So this is where the broom has gone to rest,
leaning against the shed,
its one straw wing bent to the ground,

where the rusted pick-axe, its handle lost to time,
keeps the latch-less door closed to possums and others
but mostly to wind.

No one really wants to go in there, I don't think,
lifting aside the axe which reminds me of an anchor,
the shed a battered hull that's somehow washed ashore.

Not expecting to find among the cobwebs
and shards of insect wings, the bottles of fertilizers
and poisons— on a dusty shelf in the corner—

the rainbow glow of an abalone shell,
the familiar face staring back like a forgotten lover,
patient, and slow to happiness.

SPOTTING TURKEYS

Last night's rain has flattened the grass
where a rafter of wild turkeys inches along,
      bowing as they go—
content to do just what turkeys do,
to be just who or what they are,
egg-born, bony, and humble as dirt.

They linger on the hillside with a deep thrum,
feathered instruments tuning up in bass,
assessing all in their ken:
                    glossy seedlings,
bent stalks of milkweed,
copper-green lichen on a rock,
all manner of crawling, hopping, curling,
burrowing in
      at the edges of things.

Pecking
and scrutinizing,
as if they had all the time in the world.

                        Then, crackling,
lively as fire,
      they spread across the hillside,
            darkening it with mystery.

When they leave with a low ascent
and muffled clapping, the landscape listens—
      rapt, in their spell.

YELLOW HOUSE

Yesterday, I saw for the first time
the little yellow house
with the Jacaranda in front of it,
purple petals spread about
on the sidewalk and in the branches,
although I can't say which I saw first,
house or tree.

We joined in song right away.
First the two of them,
the yellow house meting out rhythm
to the pulsing lyric of the Jacaranda,
and then the impromptu backup sighing,

Oh baby, Oh baby,
all day and all night long.

GIFTS

They've come so far to be here
this one time,
slice of a moment we notice briefly
before it passes into something else,

expecting the usual curves
they bring us, the subtle flesh scent
as we come to them, not in awe, exactly,
but more in gratitude

for how they've suddenly ripened,
for their promised sweetness,
and not especially for the shifting umbras
that help to define them

but which are still notable—
these two late and freckled pears,
gleaming on a windowsill.

THIS CUP

All through lunch I've gazed at this cup,
taking baby sips of green tea,
and now, I think,
I may be in love with it.

Glazed patches of mottled brown
and turquoise like chameleon's skin—
evidence of the enduring mutable,
set by the kiln.

Handy indentations for hands to grip,
outside and inside much the same.
On the bottom, an indecipherable
maker's name.

Crazy to love a cup, I know,
and not a wife,
but all through lunch I've been gazing
and holding on for dear life.

PRAISE FOR GRAY

There's much to be said for an overcast day.
Photographs come out better.
It gives us something to measure our sunny days by,
but who's counting?
Not the dove who wears it as an overcoat,
beating her woolen sleeves as she flies from the nest,
or the ivy leaf that bends with each drop
from the tree above.

A good day for chopping wood,
for hoisting the flag of an invisible country,
for walking up or down a hill,
for polishing shoes to a dull shine,
for baking almost anything,
especially apples.

All of which I forgo to write a poem
whose only purpose is praise for an unseen hand
that stills the air between words
and blurs the edges of the known.

CRANKING THE WHEEL
  - for my father

as I pulled in the garden hose,
I couldn't help but wonder who or what it is
that pulls us into this blooming world
and then sends us hurling into nothingness.

Or is it we ourselves who turn the wheel,
as I've done this afternoon
after flooding the rhododendron bed
with expectations of scarlet,

just beneath the window of the room
where he sleeps, all but blind now
to beauty and it's entailments.

JOICE STREET STEPS

When you climb this stair, at first it doesn't seem
a way to anywhere, although the yellow and blue
wild flowers that poke out of the mossy risers
this time of year offer their usual message of—what—
renewal? Arrival?

If you know it's there, the little altar half-way up,
you may anticipate what offerings have been given,
although there's always the fear that it may be gone
or ruined.

But it's intact and so are you—
a threadbare shelf with a few plastic flowers on it,
and an image notable more for its feeling
than its artistry, for what remains unseen.

Plainly, this is an homage to the mother of mothers
(her face could be a wing or anything living,
her face could be a prayer),
and without willing it you may find yourself

offering some silent words of praise, or thanks,
or remembrance before passing through
the airy chamber where—whose?—footsteps
have paused from the climb and what
has been stilled continues,
only lighter.

BAROMETER

It's true I no longer need you,
what with the speed of today's search engines,
air pressure and temperature at my fingertips,
but I'd still rather run them along the curve
of your mahogany casing
as you define the world in percentages and arrows,
wondering if you aren't a distant cousin of the violin,
unmusical but good with numbers,

although, I have to say, I've also wondered at times
if you weren't hiding something behind the glass,
some vital information that might be measured
by a hidden gauge that could have warned me
who would be lost early on and who would be left behind,
and another that pointed to the level of remorse
that might be expected, based on atmospheric conditions
and any number of other variables—

portents of an uncertain life, lived just the same,
surer in some small degree with you hanging there
on a wall by the door.

PULLING WEEDS

Beneath a layer of gravel and black plastic,
seeds of a meadow have poked their way
through to the light—violet stalks
topped with flaming yellow
and imperfect circles of the future
in the form of so much fluff.

                        Kneeling, I grasp each one
at the root, shaking damp earth loose,
remembering inky blackbirds
that once roosted in these ancestral weeds—
their red markings revealed
as sparks in flight—

considering just who the intruder is,
as a morning mist touches everything.

IN THE LOBBY OF HOTEL PARADISE

The orchids in the lobby are fading as fast as we are,
but appear suspended in their hexagonal basket,
woven by anonymous hands out of light and dark.
Their freshly made up faces are slightly wan
with traces of lipstick and liner,
welcoming all who come in off the street
with a wink of paradise,
what may well have been here before all this—
steel, glass, and the inevitable marble—
that and the call of "Taxi!" "Taxi!"
echoing through the air-conditioned air,
like a parrot calling for its neon mate.

LAUNDRY DAY

Standing next to the churning washer,
turning the sleeve of a shirt right side out,
I felt myself turning also—
the two of us of the same piece of cloth.

How long I stood there
and how it was that this plaid cotton shirt and I
came to be the soiled fabric of the world,
who can say?

CROW MAKES A SCENE

in the puddle where the old elm stood,
splashing and crowing for anyone who'll listen
to her chorus of wings on water, water on wings,
and the guttural praise of something wild,
unfettered.

                                        I watch as she lifts,
flying low to the ground, and circles back,
still crowing about the occurrence of water—
cool, black mirror that must be broken again,
before it takes her into its dark splendor.

STILL LIFE WITH LEMONS

Lemons in a glass bowl, centered on a white tablecloth,
could mean anything—lemonade, a lemon cake?

Someone, I think I know who, has offered them,
plucked or cut them neatly from their stems,
except for the one resting on top with its nubby cord
and double leaf like elongated butterfly wings—
like nothing you may have ever seen, except in books,
The Big Book of Butterflies, although that one had Zebra stripes
and may actually have been a moth.

What could they mean, these uncomplicated lemons,
so yellow, so waxy-perfect,
as if posing for a still-life, a gouache?
They're the flowers' answer to the same old question,
but that's side-stepping the issue, isn't it?

Are they meant for pleasure, then?
For beauty?
For their fiery seed, to turn the wheel once more?
Or are they meant for bitterness alone?

Cutting into soft rind, I inhale summer's fragrance—
sweetest clover, verbena,
                        dusty folds of marigolds—
and something almost forgotten, not yet forgotten,
in the hollow of my chest
                                exults
as if drenched in a warm rain.

PRAISING CHAIR

These days, a well-made chair is enough to give me pause,
not for its beauty exactly—
this one's all battered pine legs and peeling green paint,
but *sturdy*—

not for its beauty, per se, but for its intent,
the way it all but asks me to carry it out
into the narrow yard
where there's just enough sunlight this afternoon
to ignite brick walls,
turn camellia leaves to jade,

and I do,
finding comfort in chair, the feel of body to body,
flesh to flesh,
each of us taking on something of the other,
feet planted firmly on the ground—
not listening for the dim voices of birds in the next yard
or anything else for that matter—

leafing

VISITORS

From the great, mysterious uncertainty,
unencumbered by images of clouds
on glass hi-rises, text messages,
and broken promises,

comes the green aphid,
alighting on my wrist—all spring
with those jewel-wings
and that tiny, green body.

Friend, I've missed you!
Both of us wind borne—
you so suddenly come,
and now, gone.

EVENING RAIN

Rain sounds on the roofs of trees
and the complacent gravel,
is welcomed by everything green and ripened
coming from the ground.

It sounds the call of autumn
and just as swiftly as it comes, departs,
leaving a chorus of crickets
and this mute sighing for all that's gone—

summer moons,
scent of lemons,
the body of desire meeting itself.

Something hidden ruffles in the branches
and then, this breathing in again
for all that's fresh,

unspoken.

BONSAI

One cascades
from a mountain—
waterfall juniper.

Another frames fall
in an oval tray—
leaves staccatoed with yellow
and red, and all of them

waving in the breeze
like mismatched, shrunken
mittens.

But this one—winter pear—
miniature green fruit
cheeked with crimson,

so perfect,
so pellucid in its utility,

glows

SELF

Why not call it moonlight
between apple branches,

then find something you call
a stone or a feather

and rename it again and again,
as namer and named dissolve

in darkness, reappear
as river silt, the pale green

husk of corn, paw prints
on snow, a fox's—

all of them evading the fables
of meaning,

all of them radiant
with the moon's elixir.

FIRST FROST

This morning I feel just as if I'd stepped out of a paper sack,
staring at this glittering world with disbelief—

gessoed rooftops, sidewalks and lawns,
slickened branches, noble pines
                        and drooping bamboo,
all of them dancing with fractured light,
diamond light—

not knowing where frost leaves off and fire begins
or even what to call this
stinging bliss.

There must be hundreds of kinds of happiness
and most of us know so few of them.
Shouldn't we at least know their names?

Or if not that, act as if we do,
as if we've known them all our lives,
welcoming them with open arms when they come to us
unannounced, possibly icy and aflame,
and then watch them change, as they will,
into something else:

wisps of steam, twisting
like ghost-dancers on the rooftops;
silvered branches of the Coral Maple, seguing to red;
the silent witness, melting in rivulets
from the windowsill.

CROSSINGS

All day we waited for the ferry that never came,
the seas were too choppy, they said.
When it came the next day, dawn saw us
for what we were, not pilgrims or tourists
with the usual trappings: we were there
for the one way ticket out.

Like everyone else, we could only guess
that we would arrive safely at our destination
but where that was, exactly, I couldn't say.
Not knowing, either, that the boat would glide
so effortlessly,
like an enormous crate above the waves

that blushed pink under a starry sky,
or how quickly we would forget our names,
why we had come here at all,
if not for this boundless unknowing—the sight
of seven brown pelicans, flying in a loopy line
across our wake.

SOMETHING OF WHAT WAS

remains: this time it's the bolt
from the repaired gate
and a screw, rusted almost to oblivion.

Another time it was spectacles,
and once, letters, written in perfect script,
tied together with something like string,
kite string, or a strong twine.

The carpenter must have left them here,
unthinkingly, on the patio table—
the bolt and screw, I mean—
right next to the blackened lemon,

the one that fell weeks ago
and no one, not I,
or anyone,
knew what to do with.

Jerome Gagnon lives in the San Francisco Bay Area where he has worked as a teacher, tutor, and freelance journalist. He studied with poet Robert Creeley and novelist Kay Boyle at San Francisco State University, receiving an M.A. in English/Creative Writing. A chance encounter in his twenties with a Japanese Zen roshi led to a life-long interest in comparative religion and the sense of "suchness" that characterizes early Chinese and Japanese poetry. His poems have appeared in a variety of journals, including *Spiritus, Archaeopteryx, Poet Lore, Roaring Muse, Haiku Presence* (U.K), several anthologies, and the text, *How Higher Education Feels: Commentaries on Poems that Illuminate Emotions in Learning and Teaching.*

www.ingramcontent.com/pod-product-compliance
Lightning Source LLC
LaVergne TN
LVHW041524070426
835507LV00012B/1801